Sales 101

Sales Techniques for Beginners

© **Copyright 2014 by SIASA Ventures - All rights reserved.**

This document is geared towards providing exact and reliable information in regards to the topic and issue covered. The publication is sold with the idea that the publisher is not required to render accounting, officially permitted, or otherwise, qualified services. If advice is necessary, legal or professional, a practiced individual in the profession should be ordered.

- From a Declaration of Principles which was accepted and approved equally by a Committee of the American Bar Association and a Committee of Publishers and Associations.

In no way is it legal to reproduce, duplicate, or transmit any part of this document in either electronic means or in printed format. Recording of this publication is strictly prohibited and any storage of this document is not allowed unless with written permission from the publisher. All rights reserved.

The information provided herein is stated to be truthful and consistent, in that any liability, in terms of inattention or otherwise, by any usage or abuse of any policies, processes, or directions contained within is the solitary and utter responsibility of the recipient reader. Under no circumstances will any legal responsibility or blame be held against the publisher for any reparation, damages, or monetary loss due to the information herein, either directly or indirectly.

Respective authors own all copyrights not held by the publisher.

The information herein is offered for informational purposes solely, and is universal as so. The presentation of the information is without contract or any type of guarantee assurance.

The trademarks that are used are without any consent, and the publication of the trademark is without permission or backing by the trademark owner. All trademarks and brands within this book are for clarifying purposes only and are the owned by the owners themselves, not affiliated with this document.

TABLE OF CONTENTS

Introduction 1
Chapter 1: Get Yourself ready 2
Chapter 2: Know Your Product 11
Chapter 3: Know Your Target Market 16
Chapter 4: Know Your Client 21
Chapter 5: Winning Sales Techniques 28
Conclusion 35

Introduction

I want to thank you and congratulate you for downloading the book, *"Sales 101: Sales Techniques for Beginners"*.

This book contains proven steps and strategies on how to successfully sell your product.

This book contains the most effective techniques that you can use in communicating and introducing your product to your clients.

Starting with tips on preparing yourself, knowing your product, and your market, up to actual techniques that you can use in sales calls—this book is your ultimate guide to becoming successful in the sales industry!

Thanks again for downloading this book, I hope you enjoy it!

CHAPTER 1
Get Yourself ready

Before trying to sell anything to anybody, make sure that you are ready.

If you feel anything close to being "forced' to sell something, then you should postpone your sales call until you are sure that you want to do it.

Why? - Because every salesman becomes his product.

If you do not trust the item or idea that you are selling enough to be associated with it, then it is likely that you will not sell anything. Being in sales is a commitment to the idea that your product is the best there is and you represent it in every manner of your conduct, i.e. the way you dress, the way you speak, and the way you handle yourself.

Here are some of the ways that you can prepare yourself before selling your product.

Learn to Dress Appropriately

People rely heavily on what they see, that is why there is more focus on the visual part of a commercial than the audio.

People judge by appearance. It may not sound good, but that's the truth. Humans evolved in a way that they perceive threat or benefit best just by judging by vision.

That behavior applies to everything: what to eat, where to go, and yes, what to buy.

Your appearance is your first weapon in gaining people's trust. How to look "trustworthy"?

You do not always have to be sporting a coat and tie. Your little black dress will not score you a sale.

It is very important that you dress appropriately as the product, or the situation calls for it. Here are some examples:

1. Represent the product – If you are a part of a prime real estate company, then dress the part.

You will have to look like you own a million-dollar condominium unit, even if you don't.

If you are selling guitars, then dress casually. You do not need to dress like a hardcore metal rocker, but you will not need a suit either.

Shirt and jeans will do if you're selling anything related to musical hobbies. What if you are selling cleaning products? Do you need to be wearing overalls?

Well, of course not, if you are not doing a demo. There are other things that you need to consider when choosing your attire.

The thing called "business attire" actually depends on the business.

If you are not sure how to represent the product that you are selling, then proceed to the second example.

2. Dress according to the meeting place – Are you meeting your client in a conference room inside a corporate building?

Will you be talking to him as he plays golf with you? Are you going to discuss business with a housewife, in her house?

If you are not too sure of the best pieces to represent the product that you are selling, then choose the pieces that fit the place.

You do not want to look all "businesslike" if you're going fishing with your client—that would turn your client off.

3

Speak clearly and directly

"It is not just what you say, it's how you say it." There goes the golden mantra repeated at every communications training. In sales, the second weapon to gaining your client's trust is to "sound trustworthy".

You have to make them listen and understand what you are saying, and they would have to have a certain level of trust in you to believe what you're saying.

There are many ways to do it and you have to practice before going on a sales call.

Practicing makes it more natural, and people will trust you more if they feel that you are speaking sincerely.

1. Keep it simple – Some sales people resort to confusing their buyers if they cannot convince them.

That's a very dangerous way to deal. We are currently in the information age, and people can easily validate what you are saying in just a few seconds.

The best way to keep things simple, is to keep it real—no fluff.

The more you use technical jargon and idiomatic expressions, the more likely it is that people will turn their back on you.

People are not going to continue listening to something that they do not understand. Use simple words and as much as possible.

2. Keep it short – People have short attention spans, so keep your sentences short.

You can do this by being direct and avoiding unnecessary information. Let your audience process what you say and give them room to ask questions.

There is no use telling them every detail of your product in one long speech because they will not remember most of it.

They are likely to ask you questions about things that you already discussed after you discussed it. Why?

Because humans can only hold a certain amount of information at one time, and as they process one bit of information, they discard those that seem unimportant at that moment.

However, after processing the information, they will suddenly remember something that MAY be important, but their brain discarded the information already, and so they will ask you.

Interestingly, when they ask you a question and you answered it, they will remember the answer for a long time.

Why, you might ask. That is because they were participants in the conversation. When a person asks a question, the goal is to find the answer.

When an answer is given, it is retained because there was another process took place in the brain: forming the question.

So keeping your sentences short will allow your audience to form questions in their minds.

Do not overload them with details in one go, let them form their questions because it is likely to address their needs.

3. Enunciate your words – A part of your homework is to know the language of your clients, it will give you an upper hand because they will be able to relate to you.

However, if you do not know your client's way of speaking, be neutral. Enunciate your words to make sure that they understand you.

4. Keep a proper pace – Enunciating your words can be done without speaking too slowly. Speak too fast and you will get blank stares.

It's all about keeping the proper pace. According to studies, the proper pace is about 3.5 words per second.

Any faster than that and you will come off as too excited. Any slower will make you seem unsure or condescending.

5. Pause and use fillers – Contrary to popular belief, "uhms' and "ahs" spoken when pausing, actually help you gain people's trust.

Studies have shown that speakers who are too "smooth" sound scripted, and so buyers are not likely to trust them.

Pausing every now and then and using filler syllables make people think that you are actually thinking about what you're about to say, and not just reciting your words from memory.

Do not do it too often though because you will come off as uncertain.

6. Use anecdotes – One of the effective ways in holding people's attention is to tell a story.

It has been proven that listening to stories light up several parts of people's brains: areas responsible for smell light up when the word "stinky" is heard, those areas for the sense of touch light up upon hearing the word "rough", and areas responsible for taste light up when the word "sweet" is heard.

The more neural activity there is, the more likely it is that the experience is stored in the memory.

Stories are very effective ways to communicate. Scientists say that if you want to remember a string of random numbers, make a story connecting each number to the next one.

The power of telling stories is acknowledged by sales and marketing specialists, that is why photographers always encourage their models to "tell a story" when they are taking pictures.

This is exactly the same for face-to-face salesmanship. If you want to make sure that your client remembers the product, tell a story about it.

Not any made-up story (remember, you have to gain their trust), tell them a story that is related to you or someone you know.

Anecdotes will surely get them to listen and trust your product more because somebody else bought it.

It is better if you can provide your own story, that will give them the idea that you trust them, and so they will trust your word in return. It may sound too simple, but it works.

Build confidence

The third weapon that you can use to gain your client's trust is to "feel trustworthy".

People will look at you and say "He/She looks like someone I can trust", and then they will hear what you say and comment "He/She sounds sincere, I buy what he/she said".

However, if they sense just the slightest uncertainty in the way you handle yourself, if will all be erased and they will dismiss your business as a scam.

Aside from vision and comprehension, people rely on their instinct or "gut feeling" when deciding to buy something.

Most people will not admit it and say that they always weigh their options, but in reality, they go for what they 'feel' is right.

Because of this, they rely on their first impressions. This is the part that you have to master before selling anything.

People's first impression of you will be based on how confident they think you are.

The confident and knowledgeable you seem, the more they will trust you. Here are ways on how look and feel confident before and during a sales call:

1. Strike 'Power Poses' (before and during) – What are power poses? These are the poses made by winners and superheroes.

There exists some poses that are universally linked to winning, success, strength and confidence. Here are some of them:

a. Superhero stance – Stand with two feet about a foot apart, both hands on the hips.

b. Race Winner stance – Stand with two feet about a foot apart, both hands in the air.

c. Hugger stance - Stand with two feet about a foot apart, arms extended slightly to the side with palms facing front (as if waiting for a hug).

All three poses open the body up, so it is also important that the head is slightly raised, and the shoulders are back.

You can also do the arm poses while sitting, but sit with your legs slightly apart.

A power pose is known to create an impression of confidence.

Because it is a 'receptive' pose, it leads your audience into thinking that they can ask you anything and you'll be knowledgeable enough to answer it clearly.

Researchers showed that people who are making power poses are perceived to be more confident and more intelligent than people who have very closed body gestures.

When talking to your client, you cannot just do a Superhero, Race Winner, or Hugger stance—you will look like you're on drugs.

Instead, do something similar. Stand with your feet apart and make gestures with your hand as you talk.

This will open your body up. Make sure that the person you are talking to can always see your hands.

Interestingly, power poses do not only have effects on the audience, it also has an effect on the person doing the pose.

Scientists have recently proven that doing power poses 2 minutes before an interview or a presentation increases a person's level of confidence.

The brain releases hormones similar to what are released when people experience triumph and success.

Before a meeting, go to the washroom and make a power pose for 2 full minutes to help you feel more confident.

You can do the Superhero, Race Winner or Hugger pose (as long as nobody sees you, it's okay).

2. Smile (before and during) – One of the best non-verbal gestures that you can do to gain anybody's trust is smiling.

When a person smiles sincerely, his face "opens up". People are bound to trust someone who smiles sincerely at them.

Smiling also makes you feel confident. The Biofeedback Theory posits that when people do a positive gesture, the brain releases hormones that are related to happiness. So if you are unhappy and uncertain, smile!

In just a few minutes, you will actually feel happy and confident because of those hormones. Before meeting your client, make sure that you smile to yourself in the mirror.

3. Have a positive mantra (before) – Tell yourself that you can do it, out loud. Your confidence will stem from the belief that you can do things. If you tell yourself that you cannot sell your product to a particular client, no matter how hard you force yourself, you will not be able to make a sale.

You have to be your first buyer, your first believer. If you do not trust yourself, nobody else would.

In building your confidence, you have to hear yourself say it.

Get in front of the mirror, smile, and tell yourself that you can do it! Say it several times.

Those are not magic phrases that will automatically give you the sales you want (you still have to do the legwork), but it will definitely make you feel more confident and positive.

CHAPTER 2
Know Your Product

Companies used to separate their sales representatives from their product specialists.

They did this because the product specialists are the technical ones who do not really have time for chitchat, they only go where the problem is, analyze what happened and find the people who can resolve it.

On the other hand, the sales representatives are the ones who communicate with the client, but cannot answer any product-related question apart from what the product is for.

There is an ongoing trend of combining these two areas.

A sales representative who's also a product specialist is more likely to seal a deal and maintain the client communication.

This is what you should aim to become: someone who can talk the client into buying the product and help them in case they have technical questions.

In order to do this, you must study all the aspects of the product, even the technical ones.

Here are some of the things that you would need to know about the product that you are selling:

Study the product's history – Just as previously discussed, people love and remember stories. It is very important that you let your clients know about the history of your product and tell the story behind it.

Why was it made? Who came up with the idea? Were there any issues in making it? What were the struggles met before finally reaching the productions phase?

People will not ask for the history of the product proactively, but unconsciously, they would like to know how it is made.

Tell them the story behind what you are selling, and they'd be glad that you told them about it. Again, remember to keep your story short and avoid too much details.

Know the product's benefits – This is actually your main job. More than all the talking, looking good and being confident, knowing the benefits of your product should be your primary concern.

You have to know exactly what it is for and how it will be beneficial to your client. You have to know how it works, if you have to study the basic parts, do so.

If you have to research the science behind it, do it. Your knowledge of the product will definitely score you a thousand points to your client. Studies have shown that the first thing that people complain about when talking to sales representatives is their 'lack of knowledge about the product'.

You certainly do not want to be that person who 'doesn't seem to know anything'. You have to know everything about your product, especially its benefits.

Know the product's competition – If your product has a competition, find out everything about it.

Your clients will be armed with questions about how different your product is from other brands, and you should be ready with an answer.

Do not badmouth the competition or say anything against it that you cannot prove (unless you are ready for a lawsuit).

The way to do it is to highlight your product's advantages without saying anything bad about the competitor.

If your client says 'But this brand is a lot cheaper', tell them how your product is made from quality material.

Know the product's faults – Apart from knowing your product's high points and how it fares with other similar products, you also have to know your product's low points.

Of course, you do not volunteer this information to your client, but when the time comes that they ask you about it, let them know that you know about it and how it is being taken care of. Do not lie or make excuses.

Know your product's future – It will be very beneficial for you if you know the path that your company is heading to.

What are the plans to improve the product? Are you looking forward to creating a better version?

Knowing the vision and mission behind your product's development lets your clients know that what you are selling is a product of constant innovation and research, continuously being redeveloped to fit your client's needs.

Your company will be training you and give you all the tools you will need to know the product.

If the product has already been established, you would need to be creative in finding out people's feelings about it. Here are some of the things that you can do:

1. Check online support forums – You will be surprised to know how much opinion is poured over the Internet by consumers.

It is a known fact that nowadays, people complain about a product by posting it in social media or forums first before actually calling the manufacturer.

As a salesperson, it is your responsibility to know what the current "mood" is about the product so you can tell if it is because of actual issues, or just circulated rumors.

Most of your clients will search for online posts and forums about your product if they feel that there are things that you're not telling them, so make sure you address those issues before they find out about it themselves.

This is a preventive plan meant to keep your client's trust in you.

2. Check usual issues sent to the Customer Service department – Your company would have a customer service department meant to address the customer's concern.

Check for any common issues and FAQ's and make sure that you know the answer to them or how to resolve them quickly.

This will give you an edge over other sales people who do not seem to care about their clients after the product was purchased.

Show them that you are different and that you'll be there to assist them with any concern they may have.

3. Check out surveys – The industry that your product belongs to will have specialized publications for it.

Check for any article that provides survey results regarding your product (or the competitors) to see how your product is doing in the market.

If you are starting your own business, it is best to test your product on a handful of test clients first in order to see what they feel about it.

Here are few of the things that you can try to see which part of your product remains unknown to you.

1. Test the product yourself – You can never sell anything that you haven't tried yourself.

Your personal experience will be the best example that you can give to your clients. It adds credibility to your claim, because you'll be a living proof.

2. Have test subjects – Companies who are into selling products know that the best way to know about their product's good and bad points is to test it out with a random group of people.

You can do this too. Hand out a few samples of your products to a group of people for free or for a very low price and keep track of their usage.

It is also wise to keep case studies of the testing phase for future reference.

3. Subscribe to publications related to your industry –

Publications like magazines and journals will always have something new for you. Make sure that you are always updated with the latest news.

There may be recent studies about poisonous chemicals that you happen to use in manufacturing your product, or developments in machinery that would help you with faster production.

The information will not only be very helpful to your product, it will also make good conversation topics with your clients.

Knowing your product to the bone will make you feel confident about talking about it in front of your clients.

Confidence, as previously discussed, is perceived as one of the factors that make people trust you.

CHAPTER 3
Know Your Target Market

For beginners, people who are considered prospective buyers may look like a random group of people. In reality, it isn't.

Your target market is like a pack of wolves hunting for a specific prey.

They are individuals who have the same set of needs, and whether they know it or not, they fit into a specific demographic.

Knowing your market will help you have a general idea of the people you will be dealing with.

Determine the target market - Your company may have already done this for you. However, if you are running your own business, you have to do this yourself.

You have to have a general idea of the demographics of your market, but you also have to be open to other possibilities.

Here are some ways on how to determine your target market:

1. Know which industry your product belongs to – Is it food, fitness, hobby, or electronics?

Knowing the industry that your product belongs to will definitely help you narrow down your target market. It will let you know which part of the society will "need" the product. If you are selling a set of vitamins, for example, your industry will be health and wellness.

Health and wellness is a wide industry covering medicine, exercise, and diet. Since vitamins fall into the medicine sector of that industry, your target market will be those who are buying the vitamins.

You now have narrowed down the crowd into a group who 'want' to take vitamins and those who are 'allowed' to take vitamins (those who do not have other conditions that makes them allergic to some components of your vitamins).

Your market is not limited to the people who will actually take the vitamins, as you will learn later, but at least now you know that you cannot just sell your product to anybody.

2. Identify what problems or issues are resolved by your product – A product does not come out of nowhere. No matter what product it is, it is born out of necessity (real or created).

You would need to understand the problem and how it is negatively affecting people. Does the issue waste their time? Does the problem make them unhealthy? Are things harder for them because of the problem?

Once you understand who are affected by the problem, it would be easy to know who will be asking for solutions—they will be the ones seeking your product. Let's go back to the vitamins example.

Let's say your vitamins is formulated to help people get enough sleep. You know from the industry that there are people out there who 'want' and are 'allowed' to take the vitamins, but who are they?

The problem is lack of sleep, so your target market will be those who cannot get enough sleep: insomniacs, people who work jobs with varying time schedules, people whose biorhythms are disrupted by alcohol or caffeine, and others.

3. Identify other possible players – Your target market will not be limited to the people who directly need the product. Other players like stores and distributors will also be a part of your target market.

They will provide you with an access to a larger group of clients and they will have the names that are already associated with the product.

These other players willl actually be the ones who can give you more income in lesser amount of time.

They will become your 'muscle' and will serve as the front-liners of your products as they sell your product to the consumer directly.

Think of these people as having the same characteristics as the actual consumers—talk to them as if they will be taking your vitamin.

While some sales people think of distributors as merely 'middle men' garnering profit from added procedure, most of them actually care about the quality of the products they distribute.

They will most likely be knowledgeable about the product too and they will ask you the same questions your direct consumers would ask.

Treat them in exactly the same way as you would your direct clients.

Determine the best places where you'll find them – Aside from stores that are already selling the products that you sell, your target clients can also be seen on other venues.

Here are some of the places where you can actually find them:

1. Events and Exhibits – Trade exhibits will draw a crowd of selected people—those who are targeted by the sponsors.

Motor shows sponsored by car companies for example, draw motor enthusiasts. It is the best place for sales representatives of automotive-related products to scout.

Find any event that is related to the industry that your product belongs to, and you will find your potential clients there.

A good thing about approaching clients in these events is that it wouldn't be awkward.

Your clients will actually be expecting some sales people to offer them something while they are in that event. Keep a stack of your business cards handy.

2. Clubs and Organizations – Your product will be helping a specific group of people. It is very likely that these people will belong to an organized group.

By finding the organizations that aim to develop the industry, you will find your target market. If you are selling farming products, find the Farmers' Cooperatives names.

The members of that club will be your target clients. If you are selling health products, find clubs and organizations related to health.

The Internet has made it very easy for you to this.

3. Online Communities and Forums – the Internet has provided a virtual space where people who have the same needs and interests can meet.

Find websites, forums, blogs, and social media groups that discuss your product's industry.

Not only will you find your target clients there, you will also get a general idea of how they feel about the product.

You will see the good and bad comments that they have and it will give you a better understanding of your target market.

Legitimate online communities even schedule meet-ups in person. You can coordinate with the website administrator to see if you can get an invite.

Research possible correlations with other things

Your product belongs to an industry; that makes it related to other products within the industry.

Clever online marketers know this. That is why they provide online contents that are closely related to one another.

For example, they would have to market a cure for muscle pain.

They will create dozens of articles regarding muscle pain with keywords and links related to muscle pain relievers and therapy.

Therapy is not what the product is about, but it has something in common with medicine: it promises treatment.

The Internet is a web of connections, so this close correlation is very important.

You would have to determine which product is closely related to the one you are selling.

The people who are looking for those products will most likely be looking for your product as well, so your target market can be spotted from there.

CHAPTER 4
Know Your Client

Now that you know the general demographic, it is time to know your actual client.

Let us say you have narrowed down your prospective buyers and you have names of people that you can actually pitch your product to.

How would you know if they are going to buy from you? Is there a way to tell just by looking at them? - Unfortunately not.

Clients will be able to discern whether or not they can trust you just by the way you dress, the way you speak and the way you handle yourself. It does not work both ways though.

No matter how much you try, you will not know from the way your client dresses or the way he speaks if he is going to buy your product. Why?

It is because the ball is on their side. They are the ones who will make a decision, not you.

They are the ones who will have to weigh everything before telling you if they will buy your product.

They have the money. They will do the best they can to hide their eagerness to buy just so they can cut a favorable deal.

Do not despair though, because there are plenty of ways that you can break the barrier and know more about your client.

No, you don't have to stalk them. All you need to do is engage them in a conversation that will let them share things about themselves.

Most sales people who end up not selling anything have this misconception: *Sales is just business, everything should be formal.*

They give out checklists asking the clients about what it is that they like, and then they go out and give it to the client.

That's exactly how a government employee would treat people applying for passport or driver's license, but that is not something a good sales person will do. Successful sales people know that in order to be a winning sales agent, you should make a connection with your client.

There is no better way to make a connection than by engaging them in a personal conversation.

You would have to know things about your client, and unless you hire a private investigator, you will not know about it unless. A simpler way is to ask them directly.

3 Things Your Should Know About Your Client

Here are the 3 most important things that you should know about your clients:

1. What do they need? – However obvious it may seem, do not underestimate a client's regard for what he 'needs'. You might think, "I'm a car dealer and he called me, so it's obvious he needs a car".

Always ask them what it is that they need it for. Do they need the car because their house is too far from school? Do they need it because the one they had was wrecked because of an accident?

Ask them subtly about the story behind their need for the product. There are always some cues that you can pick up regarding the most important factors for them.

2. What do they want? – Sometimes, clients resort to buying the second-best because they cannot afford the best one. Ask them about what they really want if they do not have limitations.

Of course you cannot provide them with what they want, but will have an idea of what 'extras' they would appreciate.

You would learn later on how clients value extras and bonuses. The very act of showing interest about what they want will make them trust you even more.

3. What do they prefer? – This is the part where you give them a choice.

This will give you a hint on which aspect of the product do they value more. For example, they told you they want a white hatchback.

Ask them hypothetically which one they prefer: A black hatchback or a white sedan. This will let you know if they value color over style.

5 Ways on Effectively Communicating With Your Client

1. Ask how they want to be addressed – Start with giving your first name, then ask them if you can call them by their first name.

Nineteen out of twenty people will usually say yes to it. Why is it important?

Names have powers. In mythology and religious scripts, you would often encounter stories about dead men brought to life when their names were called, or evil spirits whose names cannot be spoken because they will wreck havoc on Earth if somebody calls them.

It is not entirely magical or supernatural.

Names excite a part of our brains that is related to attention, focus, and memory. People are wired to remember moments when their names are called, ridiculed, or praised.

Humans are also more likely to trust and follow someone who knows their name.

Calling people by last name can be viewed as formal, authoritative or respectful. Calling people by their first name can be perceived as familiar, comfortable, and friendly.

It is very important that you ask them about it first, that way you let them know that you respect their name and how they want to be called.

So every now and then, address your client by their name in your conversation. This is a very subtle way of creating a low pressure but high value environment for your sales talk.

2. Make them tell more about themselves – People like talking about themselves.

The developers of social media platforms know that very well and have amasses millions from it.

Your clients will be looking forward to the time when you will stop talking so they can say something. It may not sound so good, but it is true for everyone.

Because of this, it will work best for you if you can encourage them to tell you things about themselves.

Ask them questions about their job, their family, and their hobbies. The key is to let them know that you are interested in what they have to say.

Actually, you should be interested because this is where you'll find clues on what they want and what they need.

Be careful about questions that may be too personal for them.

If you are not sure, start by asking "I hope this is not too personal, and it's fine if you do not answer this…".

Again, it would not hurt to ask, and doing so will let them know that you respect them.

3. Point out connections— By making a good, light conversation, you are actually trying to make a connection with your client.

It is a crucial part of your sales talk because you can use the connection when you are demonstrating your product.

Do you remember from the first chapter how important personal anecdotes are? How about the 'testing the product yourself' part in the second chapter?

Those tips will not be put to good use if your clients cannot identify with you, so make sure that you point out similarities in your stories and theirs.

While your clients tell you their stories, make sure that you point out parts that you can relate to.

Simple statements like, "Really? I have a dog too" will actually trigger signals in their brains that point out familiarity.

Familiarity breeds liking. The more they can identify with you, the more they will like you.

And the more they like you, the more they will trust your anecdotes and personal accounts regarding the product you are selling.

Make sure to point out real similarities though. Do not pretend to like something you don't or make up stories just to make a connection.

Most of your clients can see through falsehoods, so you better not risk it.

People in sales are already stereotyped to be a deceitful bunch of greedy folks who lie and cheat for money, so do not prove it by being caught in a lie.

4. Make strategic compliments—Whether people admit it or not, compliments actually influence their decisions.

It has been scientifically proven that people who are complimented in a sales talk are more likely to buy from that salesman than those who are not given any compliments.

It is a very good strategy that you can employ when having a conversation with your client.

You cannot just use any compliments though, you have to acknowledge people's ability to make good actions and decisions.

Complimenting your client's appearance may come off as mere flattery meant to seduce them into buying your product. Some people would even find it inappropriate.

You do not want to come off as a honey-tongued salesperson. Instead, you want to be seen as someone who gives credit to good deeds. Compliment them on actions that they have previously done.

Make empowering statements like, "You've made a good decision there" or "That's the best way to do it" to acknowledge the fact that they did a good job.

Be subtle with your compliments and do not overuse it, unless you want them to feel like you are just saying those things to make them like you.

Like the other techniques we have discussed, do it in moderation and only when you genuinely feel like they deserve a compliment.

5. Make them say yes as often as you can—In order to 'prime' your client into saying yes to you and closing a sale, you have to condition them into saying 'yes' to you as often as possible.

You can ask them questions that can only be answered by 'yes' to drive the conversation into a positive outcome.

How will you do this? There are a couple of ways. One is to make obvious statements.

These are statements that can be confirmed easily by both of you like the weather, the environment, of traffic conditions. Sentences like "It's refreshing to have some rain earlier today, isn't it?" or "That coffee smells so good, right?" can be easily validated and if it is correct, your client will say yes to you.

Another way is to re-phrase what they said into a question. If they said, "My daughter is fourteen years old", ask them "Oh, so she is in high school now?". This will make them say yes.

Do not do this too often though; otherwise, they will think that you are not listening intently.

This is not a trick to manipulate your client. It is simply a way to condition them into agreeing with you.

Once the conversation moved into a positive mood, it is easier to get your clients to buy what you are offering them.

Now that they are starting to trust you, they are entertaining the idea that

you are the same as them.

If they feel that you are genuinely trying to get to know them and that you would like to provide them with the best service, they are more likely to agree with you and buy from you.

CHAPTER 5
Winning Sales Techniques

Now that you have prepared yourself, have studied your product, your target market and your direct client, it is time for you to employ the winning techniques of a successful sales representative.

The following are some of the psychological concepts underlying your clients behaviors and perceptions.

After each concept, a winning tip is provided for you to practice and eventually use to score your first sale.

The Principle of Reciprocity

In Physics we know that every action has an equal or opposite reaction. In Social Psychology, every individual's action towards another person implicitly solicits an equal action by the other person to the individual.

Get it? If that confused you, let us put it this way. In everything you do, you expect something of the same nature done to you. It is like a slightly distorted version of The Golden Rule.

Researchers proved that a human being do good things because they expect that good things will be done to them.

They do not consciously expect that to happen right away, but their unconscious silently takes note of it as a "debt'.

When things go south, we remember those debts and we expect those people whom we have helped in the past to help us in return.

Interestingly, the Reciprocity Principle has become so innate to human nature that the receiver of the good deed also feel indebted to the giver.

The receiver will not be conscious of it, but when the giver is in need, the receiver will feel the need to help the giver because he or she has helped in the past.

The Reciprocity Principle has helped humans survive for centuries.

As social beings, we feel tied to the idea of reciprocity that anyone who deviates to it immediately becomes an outcast.

We call them ingrates, freeloaders and other disrespectful names, just because they did not seem to understand that as human, we need to work together.

The Reciprocity Principle will help you in selling your product greatly. How?

Top Tip #1: Do Them Favors

You don't have to catch a grenade for them. You do not have to drive them home. All you need to do is give them a little token.

The Reciprocity Principle applies to any favor, big or small, it doesn't matter.

When you give something to your client, they are bound by the Reciprocity Principle to give you something in return. Some examples are:

- Give them something to drink or eat when you're talking
- When scheduling a meeting, ask them for the most convenient place and time for THEM
  Give them company souvenirs
- Open the doors for them

Remember that you only need to do simple things.

The things listed above can actually be considered as normal things that any polite person would do, but believe it or not, some sales representatives do not even try those.

Those simple things can help you win your client over, so do it. Do not do or give anything grand though, because it will look like bribery.

The Power of Touch

When a person is touched by another person, the brain secretes a hormone called oxytocin.

This hormone is dubbed as the 'bonding hormone" because it plays a major role in social recognition. It produces the feeling of relaxation and familiarity.

What did we say about familiarity again?

Yes, you remember it right: FAMILIARITY BREEDS LIKING. This is the reason why touching, when done right, feels good and comforting.

A person is more likely to forgive you if you say "Sorry" and then give him or her a hug.

A stranger is more likely to talk to you if you introduce yourself and then offer a handshake.

Some studies show that waiters and waitresses who gently touch their customers' shoulders when attending them get higher tips than those who don't make any physical contact at all.

The interesting thing is, the customers did not even take note of the fact that they were touched on the shoulder.

They were unaware of it. Such is the power of touch. It can transform the way people deal with other people in amazing ways!

So, can you use The Power of Touch when dealing with clients? The second Top Tip reveals it.

Top Tip #2: Touch Them Very Gently, Very Briefly

When introducing yourself to your client, shake their hands and slightly touch them on the arm with the other.

When having a conversation with your client, slightly touch them on the shoulder or on the arm. When walking side by side with your client, touch them on the elbow or on their back.

You have to remember that your touch needs to last 1 second at most; any longer than that would feel awkward.

You also need to remember that you have to just brush your skin very lightly, do not put any pressure.

Lastly, you have to take note of the areas that you can touch: arm, shoulder, elbow and back—nothing else.

The key is subtlety. You wouldn't want your client to feel uncomfortable with you being so 'touchy-feely'. You have to be very subtle in doing it.

The Hindsight Bias

People do not like being wrong, so whenever they are right, they need to either say it our loud or have somebody give an affirmation.

One of the biases that people have is The Hindsight Bias—also known as the "I knew It!" bias.

When people make irrational decisions based on feelings, or guesses based on their gut, and it turns out to be good, they make declarations that they knew the outcome all along.

Even though they do not have facts to back up their decision. The thing is, when the outcome is negative, they just keep silent.

People feel good when they are praised for having good instincts.

The Hindsight Bias can help you make your client feel good about themselves, and because of that, they will feel good about you.

Top Tip #3: Recognize Their Clairvoyance

When a client tells you about one of his or her lucky strikes, recognize his or her gift of guessing.

When a client tells you that "I felt that something was wrong with that car, and it turns out I'm right', agree with them and tell them they have good instincts.

If you can, back up the results with facts.

Do not make those up, just insert some facts whenever applicable. If you recognize their 'power", they will feel good about it, and will see you as an "ally".

You can then make your recommendation about the product that you are trying to sell.

The Fear of Losing

People may love the idea of winning, but the idea of losing is actually what keeps them alive. Life can be summed up by a story about a wall.

Once there was a great wall that stood between two types of landscapes. On the right is a landscape with great dangers everywhere: hungry animals, earthquakes and storms.

On the left side is a landscape of peace, green fields and everlasting happiness. In the middle is the wall where there is a little bit of everything on top of it.

There were 100 people coming from the right side when the disaster started happening.

After 5 days, the 100 people were divided into 3 groups. There are 10 people on the right side of the wall.

They tried climbing the wall but they failed, so they are now being devoured by hungry animals. They are the losers.

On the left side are the winners, and there's 7 of them alive. Ten of them climbed the wall and took the risk of jumping to the other side.

Three of them died from the fall of course, but some survived and are now enjoying a life of abundance and happiness.

Majority of the people stayed on top of the wall, there are 80 of them.

They are making ends meet, they are finding ways to grow their food, but every day, some of them are facing the dangers of wild animals and disasters too.

What's the point of the story? Some people will try and fail.

Some people will try and succeed. Some people will try, but will not try hard enough to succeed because of the fear of losing their life.

The idea of 'gaining' something is strong, but the idea of 'losing something' is much stronger.

This is the reason why people would rather be "safe than sorry".

This is the reason why most people do not take risks. They fear losing what they already have.

The concept of loss-aversion can be applied to sales, of course. The following tip demonstrates how you can use it to your advantage.

Top Tip #4: Tell Them What They'll Lose

Instead of highlighting your product's benefits by enumerating them, do it this way: Make your client imagine a scenario where they already have the product, then tell them what they will lose if they do not have the product.

When your clients already created scenes in their minds of what they are about to enjoy when they have your product, they will feel attached to it.

If they feel the threat of losing those benefits, they will most likely prevent it from happening. So what do they do to avoid losing the benefits? They'll buy the product from you.

The Bandwagon Appeal

Advertisers know this very well, and you should too. The Bandwagon Appeal is the charisma of numbers. People tend to follow the crowd, go with the 'trend', and trust the majority.

Humans and other animals survive because there is strength in numbers. It is true for the most part.

For other aspects of life like consumerism, it may not always be the best option, but nevertheless, people feel safer when they are in consensus with majority of the people.

Taking advantage of The Bandwagon Appeal is another technique that you can use when pitching your product to your client.

Top Tip #5: Give Them the Numbers

Let your client know about the number of people who already bought your product.

If this is your first sales call and you're selling a brand new product, tell them about the number of people who are MOST LIKELY going to buy the product (your target market).

It doesn't make a difference, all you need is the number. When your client hears that there are many people who bought or will likely buy your product, they will buy from you too. It's all about the numbers.

Do not lie about the numbers.

Do not make something up.

Again, you wouldn't want to be caught in a lie. All you need to do is work with the facts that you have in the most effective ways, without lying or deceiving your clients.

Conclusion

Thank you again for downloading this book!

I hope this book was able to help you to learn the techniques in becoming the best in sales.

The next step is to go out there and score that first sale! Remember that you have to gain your client's trust and you have to make a genuine connection with them. Just follow the techniques in this book and your are sure to be the best salesperson that you wanted to be!

Finally, if you enjoyed this book, then I'd like to ask you for a favor, would you be kind enough to leave a review for this book on Amazon? It'd be greatly appreciated!

Please leave a review for this book on Amazon!

Thank you and good luck!

Printed in Great Britain
by Amazon